I0285139

Original title:
Paths of Pollination

Copyright © 2025 Creative Arts Management OÜ
All rights reserved.

Author: Samuel Kensington
ISBN HARDBACK: 978-1-80566-716-2
ISBN PAPERBACK: 978-1-80566-845-9

Colorful Invitations

The daisies dressed in bright flair,
Sending signals through the air.
"Come one, come all to the green fest,"
Their petals wave, they want the best.

The tulips giggle, "Look at me!"
In their best shades of jubilee.
"Let's throw a bash, with nectar galore!"
While bumblebees shake their dance on the floor.

In Search of the Sweet

A plucky bee with a tiny hat,
Buzzed with a grin, feeling quite fat.
"I'm the king of this flower feast!"
"Gimme the nectar, I want the least!"

With clumsy hops and a jolly spin,
He dived into petals, with a big grin.
"Oh my, what a sticky day!"
"But hey, who cares? It's a sugary play!"

The Whispering Flora

Whispers exchanged in the gentle breeze,
Petals shake hands and giggle with ease.
"Did you hear what the lilies said?"
"Nectar's a party, let's go, let's spread!"

The roses rolled their eyes in glee,
"Oh please, not another bee on a spree!"
But they all knew it was quite a catch,
As they signed up for the nectar batch.

Harmony Among the Blossoms

In the garden of laughter, all is bright,
The flowers sway under the sunlight.
"Dance with me, my colorful friends!"
"Let's laugh and play till the day ends!"

With every buzz, a chance to cheer,
Each bloom has a joke for the busy sphere.
"Why do flowers do the cha-cha?"
"Because they love to sway, oh la la!"

Whispers of the Bumblebee

In a garden bright and sunny,
A bee with dreams, and not much money,
Buzzes round with all his glee,
Searching high for that sweet fee.

He asks a flower, 'What's the buzz?'
'Got nectar?' she replies with fuzz,
He jigs and wiggles, quite the sight,
A pollen party, what a flight!

Nectar Trails in Bloom

Flitting here, then zooming there,
Bees sign contracts with fragrant flair,
'I'll trade you pollen for this treat,'
Said Daisy, 'You can't miss this sweet!'

A rose pipes up, with petals wide,
'Join us for a floral ride!'
A honeyed bumble, quite the tease,
Found his way 'tween groovy leaves!

The Dance of Daisies and Bees

In a field where daisies gleam,
Bees groove to a nectar dream,
Twirling 'round, they shake their wings,
Buzzing tunes like tiny kings.

Daisy whispers, 'Here, take some!'
While Bumble bumbles, 'Oh, I'm done!'
They sway and jig, in pure delight,
A pollen dance that feels so right!

Fluttering Journeys of the Heart

Through fluttery paths, they race and spin,
Each bloom a game, let the fun begin!
They trade their smiles, a floral exchange,
A light-hearted journey, oh, so strange!

With laughter sweet, and petals ripe,
Bees swish and swirl, a lively type,
In this garden, where joy takes flight,
Hearts bloom bright, in noon's warm light!

Secrets in the Breeze

There's a tiny bee with a big ol' grin,
Zipping past flowers in a dandelion spin.
He whispers sweet nothings to every bloom,
While sneaking a snack in the midday gloom.

A ladybug chuckles, her polka dots bright,
"Why don't you come join my garden delight?"
They share a good laugh as they dance in the sun,
Mixing their giggles with nectar and fun.

The Garden's Journey

Two ants on a picnic, oh what a sight,
Carrying crumbs that are bigger than light.
They wobble and giggle, so clumsy and spry,
"Who needs a lunchbox? Let's just share the pie!"

A butterfly flutters, she can't help but grin,
"Did you hear the buzz? Let the feast begin!"
With each tasty morsel, the garden's alive,
Making a ruckus, making friends thrive!

Wings of the Voyager

A moth with a map and a bee with a plan,
Set off for adventures, the best they can.
"Let's find the juiciest petals around,"
Said the moth, with a laugh, spinning round and round.

They dodged all the raindrops, they giggled and soared,
Caught in the thrill of a sweet nectar chord.
In every bright color, they found their own place,
Turning the garden into a big party space!

Sunlit Trails of Sweetness

A bumblebee's laugh is a bubbly delight,
As he buzzes past sunflowers, oh what a sight!
"Hey, why is the clover so lucky?" he said,
"Because it's got four leaves and a gang full of thread!"

As petals applaud in their riotous glee,
A squirrel grabs an acorn, saying, "Wait for me!"
Together they dance, in the light of the moon,
Crafting a melody, the garden's own tune!

In the Garden of Dreams

In a garden where whispers bloom,
Bees wear tiny hats, zoom-zoom!
Flirting with flowers, quite the scene,
Dancing in circles, looking so keen.

Butterflies gossip, sipping on tea,
'Did you see Jim? He's stuck in a tree!'
Ladybugs giggle, rolling in grass,
While ants play charades, oh what a gas!

The tulips blush, they can't help but sway,
'Who knew the sun could throw such a ray?'
While daisies tickle each bumblebee's nose,
Laughter erupts, as friendship grows!

So come take a stroll, through colors and cheer,
Where nature's the star, and joy is near.
Forget all your worries, just let it be,
In this funny garden, so wild, so free!

Life's Interwoven Patterns

In gardens, bees dance with glee,
Chasing a bloom for its sweet decree.
Butterflies flit with their sparkly flair,
While ants munch crumbs without a care.

Daisies whisper to the tall grass,
"You thought you'd hide? We'll let that pass!"
Worms in the soil, having a ball,
Say, "Party's here! You can't miss it all!"

A Rhapsody in Bloom

Pollen swirls like a confetti blast,
Bees wearing leg warmers, moving fast.
Ladybugs gossip, enchanting the trees,
"I saw him first!" - a quirk in the breeze.

Hummingbirds hum their zippy tune,
Mocking the flowers, "You'll bloom up soon!"
Squirrels are dodging, playing tag quick,
While flower pots laugh, quite the comedic flick!

In the Heart of Spring

Buds come alive in a clumsy feat,
Clouds tussle over who'll bring the heat.
Gophers peek out, checking the vibe,
While daisies giggle, forming a tribe.

Rabbits jump in, a joyful parade,
Each step they take, a hop and a fade.
Honeybees strategize, plotting their flight,
"Pollinate, don't hesitate! What a delight!"

Threads of Golden Dust

There's a dandelion puff, feeling grand,
Waving its seeds like a tiny band.
Grasshoppers plan a quick game of leap,
"Catch the pollen!" they chirp, never sleep.

Flies with sunglasses zoom in style,
While ants form lines, talking all the while.
Caterpillars munch, thinking it's rare,
"Who knew dining could be filled with flair?"

Journeys of Color and Life

Bees in tiny tuxedos dance,
Buzzing like they own the chance.
With pollen pots strapped on tight,
They twirl around, such a sight!

Flowers giggle, what a show!
"Do the bee," they chant below.
A clumsy ant joins for the ride,
Spilling pollen, what a glide!

Sweet nectar pools in the sun,
Bees chase each other, oh what fun!
Bouncing blooms with laughter sound,
Nature's circus all around!

So here's a toast to their ballet,
Colorful, wild, a bright display.
With wings so wide and hearts so free,
Life's a party, come and see!

Wings Over Nectar Streams

A hoverfly with shades of pink,
Drinks from flowers, stops to think.
"Is this the place? Where's my mate?"
He spins in circles – such a fate!

Dragonflies with acrobatic flair,
Flipping and flopping, oh do beware!
They zig and zag in the golden beam,
"I just want nectar!" one does scream.

Bumblebees in a band unite,
Playing tunes from day till night.
Their rhythm makes the blossoms sway,
Nature's music, come out and play!

Each sip stolen, oh the glee,
Life is sweeter when you're free.
So dance and flutter, loop the loop,
With wings like these, we form a troop!

A Bouquet's Secret Messengers

In a garden where whispers bloom,
A ladybug skips with room.
She's on a mission, oh so bold,
Delivering secrets, tales untold!

Butterflies wearing coats so bright,
Saunter through the soft twilight.
"I'm not just pretty, I can chat!"
Fluttering gossip, what's up with that?

They gather round like friends at noon,
Talking of love beneath the moon.
"Who's taking nectar from my stash?"
A drama unfolds – oh, what a clash!

But with a wink and a pollen gift,
They make amends, sweet relations shift.
In this bouquet, fun never ends,
Nature's jesters, all good friends!

The Gentle Touch of Nature's Artists

With a stroke of their tiny brushes,
Creatures create as the world hushes.
Petals painted in electric hues,
Nature's art, delightful news!

A solitary bee, quite aloof,
Tries to make its own little spoof.
Dancing solo like a star,
"Look at me! I'm born to spar!"

Flits of butterflies, stunning grace,
Each move a careful, swirly trace.
They land with giggles, sharing snacks,
Pollen smeared – what a fun mix-up!

And as they frolic, spread the cheer,
Nature's jokers are always near.
With colorful splashes everywhere,
Life is a canvas, without a care!

Bees and Blossoms: An Endless Quest

Buzzing round in a frantic race,
With pollen puffs, they take their place.
A daisy's call, a tulip's grin,
They zig and zag, it's a pollen win!

Chasing petals like tiny fools,
With sticky legs, breaking the rules.
A flower's wink, a butterfly's jest,
In this sweet chase, who's the best?

Bound by Nectar, Free in Flight

They flit and flutter, oh what a sight,
Stuck in syrup, yet feeling light.
Trapped on a bud, with laughter so loud,
"Excuse me!" they yell, "We're pollinator crowd!"

A clumsy bump, a tumble so bold,
In sun-kissed fields, their stories unfold.
With every sip, they pull a prank,
What's sweeter than honey? Oh, the laugh tank!

Calendar of Seasonal Companions

When spring arrives, the bees can't wait,
Their pollen parties, such fine fate.
In summer's shine, they take to the sky,
"Who knew nectar could make us fly?"

Fall brings a chill, but they don't flee,
"Maybe we'll hibernate, or sip some tea!"
Winter's frost, fun's on hold,
"Cuddle up tight, and share the gold!"

Dances under the Sunlit Canopy

In the garden's groove, they bust a move,
With petals as partners, they find their groove.
A sudden sway, a flower's twirl,
"Watch out!" they say, "Here comes the whirl!"

Around they spin, a dizzy delight,
Under sunbeams, everything feels right.
With laughter buzzing, they paint the scene,
As they partner up, so wild and keen!

Nature's Lullaby

In the garden, bees do dance,
Sipping nectar, taking a chance.
Flowers giggle with vibrant hues,
Winking at the buzzing news.

Under the sun, they play peekaboo,
Petals flutter like a dance crew.
Drunk on pollen, bees take their flight,
Spreading laughter in morning light.

A butterfly in a dapper suit,
Whispers secrets to a sleepy root.
Rainbows spark in a gentle breeze,
Nature's whimsy makes hearts freeze.

Then the ladybugs join the fun,
Rolling 'round till the day is done.
In this chaos, joy's the key,
Every bloom buzzing with glee.

Charmed Circles

Bees wear hats, oh what a sight,
Pollinating with sheer delight.
Buzzing jokes as they flit about,
Spreading smiles, there's no doubt.

Daisies whisper to the sun,
"Why don't you join us? It's more fun!"
Lilies laugh in a flood of bright,
Creating scenes of pure delight.

A bumblebee trips, oh what a fall,
Stumbles right into a daffodil ball.
Tulips snicker as they sway,
"Look at him dance, hip-hip-hooray!"

The sun sets low, the stars appear,
Nature's jokes all with cheer.
In circles, they twirl with glee,
Blossoming joy, wild and free.

Ethereal Embrace

In twilight's glow, fairies play,
Whispering secrets, come what may.
Honeybees wear their tiny crowns,
Making music with sweet sounds.

The flowers spin in a waltz so grand,
With dewdrops glistening, hand in hand.
As butterflies swoop and swerve,
Nature's jesters, oh how they serve!

A frantic squirrel jumps with flair,
Dressed in leaves beyond compare.
He chuckles loudly at a flower,
"Don't you wish you had this power?"

As night time falls, the fireflies wink,
Painting the air with a playful link.
Together they twirl, in harmonized pace,
Embracing the night in a coy space.

Fables of the Flowers

Once there bloomed a sunflower wise,
With a grin that reached the skies.
Telling stories of a daring bee,
Who fancied herself a grand marquee.

Roses rolled their fragrant eyes,
"Dare she dream of such a prize?"
While pansies poked their cheery heads,
"Let's have a giggle before bed!"

The blossoms laughed till dusk was near,
In this garden, joy was clear.
Each petal whispered tales untold,
Of moments sweet and antics bold.

And as the stars began to shine,
In every heart a spark divine.
With every flower, a tale anew,
For life's a play, and we're the crew.

A Tapestry of Flavor

In gardens bright where colors bloom,
Buzzing friends zoom room to room.
With every sip, sweet laughter flows,
As bees in tiny costumes pose.

They swirl and twirl, a merry sight,
Dressed in yellow, oh so bright!
A grand parade of pollen feasts,
Where nectar's rich, the party's least.

Flowers giggle in the sun,
As petals wave, they're having fun.
With each tiny drop, a flavor's born,
A banquet spreads each early morn.

So raise a glass, give bees a cheer,
For all their work throughout the year!
From fruit to flower, the magic's done,
In this tasty dance—everyone's won!

Beneath the Canopy

Under trees where dandelions sway,
A buzzing gang starts their play.
With mischief in their little wings,
They aim for blooms, oh what joy it brings!

They dip and dive, a quirky crew,
Spilling pollen like confetti, too.
"Oops!" they shout, "We spilled the prize!"
As butterflies laugh, they roll their eyes.

In a world where nectar glows,
They barter jokes and sweetened prose.
With each light gust, their laughter trails,
A symphony of wings, their happy tales.

So when you see them on a spree,
Know beneath the leaves, it's jubilee!
Pollinators in a playful huddle,
Creating sweetness through all the muddle!

The Route of Radiance

On sunny days, they plan a route,
With giggles loud, you can hear them shout.
To flowers dressed in finest hues,
They zoom and dance, this crew of snooze!

Each bee a captain, a guide on high,
Leading their friends through the open sky.
"Don't miss this one!" a bee will call,
As daisies sway, having a ball.

The blossoms sway to the buzzing beat,
While ants cheer up from their tiny seat.
The pollen party's just begun,
With extra sprinkles, life's so fun!

So if you see them bask in rays,
Know they're just counting their silly days.
A map of colors leads the way,
In laughter's arms, they spend their play!

Dance of the Honeymakers

In twilight's glow, they take the stage,
With honey dreams, they set the page.
They twist and spin on floral floors,
A buzzing ballet, who could ask for more?

With each pirouette, they steal the show,
Their golden gowns, like rays that glow.
"Let's do the waltz!" a brave one calls,
While others giggle, tripping, taking falls.

They bump and grind, all in good cheer,
With tiny legs, they dance sincere.
Each drop of honey fuels the fun,
A sticky joy that's second to none.

So join the dance beneath the stars,
With pollen medals, no fading scars.
The honeymakers' jive is quite the sight,
A honeyed lifetime wrapped up tight!

Pollinator's Perch

Bees in bow ties buzz with flair,
Dancing round flowers without a care.
While butterflies in shades so bright,
Do a waltz in the warm daylight.

Sipping nectar with every spin,
They laugh as petals make them grin.
The ladybugs cheer, their tiny seats,
For each pollen party they all meet.

Hummingbirds zip with a playful tease,
Darting 'round as if at ease.
It's a wild show, nature's delight,
With critters partying from day to night.

Veins of Vitality

Roots underground, sipping from cups,
While flowers giggle as the sun erupts.
Wiggly worms give a comedic nod,
Planting seeds for the future, oh so odd!

With starlings singing a funky tune,
Swaying along beneath the moon.
The daisies tell jokes, their petals sway,
As bees reply, 'We're here to play!'

Tiny ants march in a silly line,
Gathering treats, a feast so fine.
"Who ordered this?" chuckle the caterpillars,
As they munch on leaves, the nature thrillers!

The Song of the Senses

Frogs croak out a rhythmic beat,
While crickets chirp in a grand seat.
With flavors twirling and scents ablaze,
The garden hums in a joyous craze.

Whiffs of rosemary twirl with delight,
As cinnamon butterflies take flight.
Buzzy bees bring their own sting,
Hilarity reigns in this lively spring!

Silly snails race with such slow grace,
Tripping over traits that they embrace.
In this circus of color and song,
A funny spectacle where all belong!

Starlit Paths of Bloom

Under a sky where fireflies shine,
Dance the petals, they're feeling fine.
With a twinkle up high and a giggle below,
They sway like a train, a floral show!

The nocturnal creatures join the spree,
Mice in tuxedos, oh so fancy!
As raccoons tap dance in playful charm,
While the garden hums with a magical balm.

Pollen floats like confetti in air,
Critters unite without a care.
The night blooms bright, a sight to cherish,
In laughter's embrace, these joys won't perish!

Pollen Drifts in Sunlit Meadows

In meadows bright, where flowers play,
   The buzzy bees are here to stay.
  They dance on blooms, a silly sight,
While butterflies laugh, taking flight.

A bumblebee wearing a crown,
Stumbles in petals, falls right down.
He shakes it off, with sass and glee,
His little buzz—"Come dance with me!"

  The daisies giggle, the lilies cheer,
The grass gets tickled, oh dear, oh dear!
They share a joke, the sunbeam's bright,
  While daisies sway in pure delight.

With nectar sweet and pollen galore,
They party on 'til their wings are sore.
These meadows laugh, in joyful ways,
  As nature shines through sunny days.

Scented Breezes and Winged Embraces

In scented breezes, whispers pass,
With wings a-flutter, oh, what a class!
A ladybug sports a tiny hat,
While flitting by, the ants all chat.

The hummingbird, so zippy and spry,
Zooms past a flower with a wink of the eye.
"Hey there, cutie, I'm here for a sip!"
He swirls around, on nectar, he's hip.

Two dragonflies play tag in the sun,
Zooming and darting, it's all in good fun!
They giggle and laugh, with wings in a twirl,
While flowers sway and the breeze gives a whirl.

Bumblebees bustle, quite chummy they are,
Sharing their secrets, and never too far.
They hum about joy, not a worry in sight,
In their winged embrace, everything feels right.

Yellow Dust upon the Petals

Oh, the yellow dust that gets around,
A sprinkle here, a sprinkle sound.
The bees go marching, so proud, so bold,
With stories of flowers, they happily told.

A pollen party, what a scene!
Fluttering about, they swirl in between.
One bee slips, falls right in a bloom,
"I meant to do that!" he cries with a zoom.

A butterfly lands, brushing gold,
On dewy petals, it's a sight to behold.
But wait! There's a sneeze, in the breeze it goes,
The petals giggle, while everyone knows!

With yellow dust upon their backs,
They race through fields on their merry tracks.
These flowers giggle, in sunny delight,
As bumbles and buds whirl in pure flight.

Vibrant Routes of Nature's Couriers

The couriers flit, with bags on the go,
Spreading their joy, putting on a show.
Each flower waits, a giggle to share,
As a buzzing friend arrives, filled with care.

A butterfly winks, all decked in bright,
"I just flew here! What a lovely sight!"
Petals whisper secrets, soft and low,
While the sunbeam dances, putting on a glow.

With a flurry of wings, they argue and tease,
"I see more blooms, let's hurry, please!"
They zip and zoom, in a dizzying race,
Nature's couriers, with smiles on each face.

At dusk, they settle, tired but spry,
Sipping sweet nectar with a contented sigh.
In vibrant routes, they spread the cheer,
These messy, lovely couriers, we hold dear.

Beeswax Roads to Hidden Gardens

Buzzing along on a golden spree,
With pollen backpacks, such sights to see.
Dancing on flowers, a whimsical sight,
They steal the sweet nectar, oh what a delight!

Tiny legs stuck in sticky mess,
Their little antennae, they try to impress.
With rainbow dust, they frolic and play,
Creating confusions in their busy ballet!

They zigzag like dancers on a stage,
With no time to stop, they're filled with rage.
'What's my next stop?' they ponder in flight,
A map made of blossoms, their pure delight!

Each flit is a giggle, each buzz is a cheer,
The garden's a playground, filled with good cheer.
Through fields of bright blooms, they skip and they hop,
Beeswax roads lead them, they never will stop!

The Symphony of Flight and Fragrance

In the orchestra of blooms, they take their stand,
Wings whirring like violins in command.
A double bass buzz adds to the tease,
With each drift and dive, they play as they please!

Dandelions whistle as they do their dance,
Chasing sweet scents as if in a trance.
But oh! Watch your step, or you'll trip and fall,
Into a pile of petals, oh what a ball!

With a flick and a flap, they steal the show,
A honeyed duet from high to below.
The blooms all applaud as they whirl and twirl,
This fragrant parade, oh what a swirl!

No conductor needed, they're all in the groove,
In this lively sweet concert, they can't help but move.
From rosebud to lily, what joyous refrain,
A symphony created through laughter and gain!

Pollinators' Serenade

In the garden's embrace, they make quite a fuss,
Jiving and buzzing, creating a plus.
With a footloose drop-in and a twirly spin,
Every flower's a partner, let the waltzing begin!

Oh, the lilacs are laughing, they tickle the nose,
While daisies giggle, striking silly poses.
They share little jokes in the sunlight so bright,
Unfolding their petals, what a sight!

As each critter flutters, they can't help but sing,
A melody crafted from the joy they bring.
Shaking the pollen right off their fine coats,
Filling the air with their sweet little notes!

In their cheerful world, there's kindness and glee,
With every fond buzz, they spread love like a spree.
To the rhythm of nature, they dance and they sway,
A serenade to keep worries at bay!

Echoes of Sweetness Among the Flowers

In the whispers of petals, a giggle takes flight,
Honeyed echoes buzz through morning light.
With wiggly wiggles, and a hilarious glide,
They scoot from bloom to bloom, filled with pride!

A bumblebee jokes with a butterfly friend,
'Let's see who can land at the highest end!'
With each playful nudge, they uplift the day,
Creating sweet stories along the way!

Sunshine is smiling, as colors collide,
While critters in laughter humorously glide.
With nectar as currency, they barter and trade,
Riding on gusts, a rollicking parade!

Amidst nature's canvas, a vibrant delight,
Sweet echoes of friendship spark joy in the light.
Through fluttering hearts and a dash of sweet cheer,
They pen the best stories for all to endear!

Echoes of Emergence

Buzzy bees in a crazy flight,
Dodging flowers, oh what a sight!
Hiccups from sipping the sweet,
Stumbling back on their little feet.

Ladybugs laugh, they roll and bounce,
While ants play tag, they poke and pounce.
A sunflower grins, feeling a bit tall,
As petals sway in a jovial sprawl.

Winds whisper jokes, rustle leaves just right,
A butterfly flaps, joins in the delight.
Each bloom giggles, as friends all join,
In this dance, with nectar they coin.

The Quest for Nectar

In search of the sweet, the buzzing crew,
With sticky wings and a vibrant hue.
They flit and flutter, oh what a race,
Every droplet's worth a joyful embrace.

One bee gets stuck, oh what a fail,
Dancing on petals, like a little snail!
While flowers chuckle, their colors bright,
"Keep sipping, friend, you'll get it right!"

They barter for pollen, trade it with glee,
"Oh no, that's mine!" says a tiny bee.
With every sip, they toast to the fun,
In this quest, surely everyone's won!

Bound by the Breeze

The wind carries whispers, a mischievous tease,
Tickling the petals, swaying the trees.
Bumblebees wobble, and daisies spin round,
While squirrels make funny faces, spread joy all around.

A butterfly drifts, then suddenly dives,
Chasing a floating, colorful hive.
"Hooray for the breeze!" they all shout aloud,
As scents mingle sweetly, like laughter in a crowd.

Grasshoppers hop in a comical line,
Determined to join this messy design.
Every creature smirks, as chaos unfolds,
Bound by the breeze, in sunshine of gold.

A Dance in the Sunlight

Under the sun, all the insects prance,
In every corner, you'll spot a chance.
Flies with their jazz, they spin and they sway,
While ants tap their feet, joining the display.

Petals wave, sharing secrets, so bright,
Colors collide in the warm, gentle light.
With every buzz, they start a new game,
"Come one, come all, let's dance without shame!"

Laughter erupts as they tangle in fun,
A mix of pure joy, old and young.
From flower to flower, they twirl through the day,
A raving, buzzing, sunlit ballet.

The Infinite Circle of Life's Flavor

A bee in a tutu dances with glee,
Buzzing and weaving, oh look at me!
Pollen on her nose like a badge of pride,
She twirls through the blossoms, can't be denied.

The ants in their hats march in straight lines,
Carrying crumbs, laughing at signs.
A ladybug winks, it's all quite absurd,
In this wacky garden, they've spread the word.

The flowers are giggling, petals like cheer,
Each bloom is a party, come join the sphere!
Colorful confetti thrown from the sky,
Nature's own circus, oh my, oh my!

From seedling to sprout, it's a comical chase,
Every critter dances, each finds their place.
Life's a hoot, in this floral delight,
Grab some popcorn, let's watch it take flight!

Melodies of Springtime's Pollinators

Bumblebee beats his drum with delight,
While butterflies flutter, a colorful flight.
A cricket croons softly, the leaves tap their feet,
In this garden concert, it's hard to compete.

The hummingbirds swoosh, like tiny balloons,
Sipping nectar to sweet, jazzy tunes.
Everyone's jiving, beneath the sun's glow,
With blossoms as fans cheering 'go, go, go!'

A caterpillar croons while munching his leaf,
In a world full of laughter, there's never grief.
Nature's own symphony, tuneful and bright,
In the bliss of springtime, oh what a sight!

So chuckle and sway with this vibrant crew,
A chorus of colors, each note feels brand new.
Join in the fun, let your spirit take wing,
In the melodies made by the flutter and fling.

A Tapestry of Color and Connection

In gardens of laughter, where colors collide,
Dandelions giggle, with petals so wide.
A rascally rabbit hops past with a wink,
In a world of connection, they all stop and think.

Bees sporting capes buzz by in a hurry,
While ants play the conga, no time to worry.
Lizards do ballet on sun-warmed rocks,
And ladybugs gossip, sharing their flocks.

With splashes of yellow, pink, and bright blue,
Each creature a stitch in this grand quilt anew.
The sun's a great painter, soft strokes of light,
Creating a canvas, both cheerful and bright.

So wander through gardens, explore every hue,
Each petal a tale, every creature's a clue.
In this wacky place where the wild things roam,
Life's colorful fabric welcomes you home!

Heirlooms of the Garden's Keepers

Nectar on his nose, a bumblebee chef,
Stirring up sweetness, no need for the rest.
His spatula's tiny, but he cooks with flair,
Crafting fine delicacies with a buzz in the air.

A squirrel in boots, with a flair for the bold,
Stealing the seeds, oh that little scold!
He twirls with mischief, a nut in each hand,
Making a ruckus in this lively land.

The flowers stand guard, with their colors so bright,
Throwing a banquet under warm sunlight.
With petals like plates and dew drops like wine,
Every critter giggles, it's a feast so divine!

So raise up your glasses, let's toast to the crew,
In this garden of heirlooms, where laughter is true.
With whimsy and wonder all tangled in play,
Join the festivities—come on, let's sway!

Fluttering Stories in the Air

A bumblebee danced on a daisy,
Spinning tales, oh so crazy.
With a sprinkle of pollen flair,
It made all the flowers stare.

Butterflies flit with fairy wings,
Whispering secrets of funny things.
They giggle at petals, so bright and bold,
Silly stories of nectar to be told.

Ladybugs laugh in a dotty way,
Joking about the sun's warm ray.
Gathering round, they form a crew,
Planning the sweetest rendezvous.

Hummingbirds hum their spirited tune,
Dancing beneath the glowing moon.
In this garden, mischief reigns,
As nature bursts with joyful gains.

Sweet Currents in the Floral Realm

In a meadow where giggles flow,
Nectar pools like a sugary show.
Bees dive in, with buzzing fun,
Competing for sips, like it's a run!

Petals whisper in the breeze,
Tickling bees as they aim to please.
With each sip, a chuckle shared,
In this world, sweet jokes are aired.

Grasshoppers hop with a comic spring,
Cracking jokes while the flowers swing.
They leap and bound in nature's play,
Causing giggles to chase petals away.

Sunflowers rise like bright-faced clowns,
Cheering up the bumbles in town.
Smiling wide, they take the stage,
In this floral realm, laughter's the wage.

The Language of Bloom and Wing

Petals flutter in a chirpy prose,
Comics of colors, in laughter, they pose.
Bee banners wave in the sunny light,
Telling tales of joy, oh what a sight!

Wings are flapping like eager hands,
Sharing gags from whimsical lands.
Blossoms blush as they hear the joke,
In the comic air, no spirits choke.

A firefly winks with a bright little grin,
While a ladybug chuckles and joins in.
Nature's drama unfolds with cheer,
Each buzz and flutter brings warmth near.

As flowers bloom, laughter entwines,
In a language that's silly, nothing confines.
With each playful jest, the world's delight,
In every corner, sprightly and light.

Nature's Voids and Vibrant Fills

In the garden, there are gaps to fill,
Where flowers giggle and beans give thrills.
Buzzing friends come to take their place,
With each little joke, they spark the space.

A butterfly's dance, oh, what a tease,
Twirling through blooms with graceful ease.
Meanwhile, a flower trip is unplanned,
As petals tumble, laughter unspanned.

The ants hold meetings, they plot and scheme,
While ladybugs burst with a chuckling dream.
Together they fill nature's empty sights,
Creating a show of sprightly delights.

As the sun dips low, joy doesn't cease,
Nature's voids filled with giggles and peace.
In this wild world, where fun takes flight,
Every bloom and wing paints the night bright.

The Enchanted Trail

In a garden so bright, I tripped on a vine,
A bee buzzed by, said, "Hey, take your time!"
With pollen in pockets, they danced through the air,
While I just stood still, tangled in hair.

A dandelion chuckled, "You've got quite the flair!"
All the flowers giggled, in colors so rare.
With each little stumble, a chuckle arose,
And the ants looked amused, in their tiny clothes.

The sun began setting, a golden parade,
As I chased fluttering wings, in this charm they made.
They zapped by my ear with a spark and a grin,
I waved at a butterfly, as it twirled in.

But when I lost balance and fell in the dirt,
They laughed as I tumbled, shouting, "Oh, what a flirt!"
So I rolled with the punch, and along with the bees,
In this whimsical chaos, at last, I found ease.

Petal by Petal

A honeybee winks, with a sweet little buzz,
"Hey there, dear flower, don't give me a fuzz!"
I watched as each petal opened with style,
The blooms threw a party! It lasted awhile.

They danced in the breeze, just a little bit coy,
While I tried to keep up, feeling rather like soy.
Buzzing with laughter, petals twirled all around,
Then dipped into nectar, a feast that they found.

I tripped on a leaf, what a comical sight!
The tulips began laughing; oh, what pure delight!
With vines overhead, the daisies took aim,
And tossed little raindrops like they were a game.

But I laughed right along, in this brilliant ballet,
Where flowers were jesters, and I was the play.
So round and around, like a merry-go-round,
Just a curious human in a garden unbound.

Glimmers of Growth

A seed hoped for sunshine, while sleeping so tight,
It dreamed of the sky, oh, what a delight!
Suddenly, a worm poked its head through the dirt,
"Wake up! There's a party! Come join us, you squirt!"

With sprouts all around, they chattered in glee,
"Let's grow taller together, just follow me!"
I chuckled a bit at this leafy parade,
As the radish complained, "My leaves are mislaid!"

The daisies were dancing; I asked to take part,
They said, "Just grow taller, it's a work of art!"
So I stretched and I groaned, matching their fun,
While even the weeds knew we'd all soon be one.

In this whimsical chaos, I felt quite at home,
Among giggles and wiggles, in green I did roam.
And by the time evening came, stars twinkled bright,
We laughed through the darkness, all merry and light.

The Secrets of the Sweets

In a garden of wonders, I met a sly bee,
"Have you heard all the gossip? Come sip tea with me!"
The blossoms exchanged whispers, all sweet like honey,
"If you dance with us now, it'll be really funny!"

The lilacs all giggled, while the roses rolled eyes,
As petals spun stories underneath sunny skies.
"Last week, a butterfly wore a hat too big,"
"And tripped on a petal, oh me, oh my, what a jig!"

The daisies spread tales of a lazy old snail,
"He tried to run a race and ended up pale!"
So I joined their sweet laughter, my troubles disappeared,

In the folds of their petals, my joy was endeared.

With a sprinkle of nectar, and laughter galore,
The world felt so vibrant, who could ask for more?
We danced in the sunlight, a quirky little fleet,
In this garden of gossip, where laughter's the treat!

Sweet Symphony of Life

In gardens green, the buzz we hear,
A dance of wings, with no hint of fear.
Bees chase their dreams, while flowers laugh,
Sipping on nectar, a sweet epitaph.

A clumsy ant took to the sky,
On a daisy petal, oh me, oh my!
Sipped too much nectar, oh what a sight,
Hitching a ride on a butterfly's flight.

Wiggling worms in a wiggly line,
Singing a song, "Hey, it's pollinator time!"
These tiny friends in a chaotic swirl,
Making the magic in this great big world.

When pollen flies like confetti thrown,
Every bloom smiles, their colors grown.
In this funny garden, no need to flee,
Life's sweet symphony, just let it be!

Beyond the Horizon of Petals

A bee on a mission, wearing a hat,
Swirling around like a zany acrobat.
A flower shouts, "There's pollen today!"
The bee buzzes back, "No time to play!"

Butterflies giggle in the brightly lit air,
On a quest for the finest, without a care.
One slipped and landed in a soup of dew,
With a flurry of wings, "Now what do I do?"

The sunflowers wave in a friendly cheer,
As the ants march on, "Hey, we're here!"
They scurry about with the utmost pride,
Turning up noses, as if like a guide.

Beyond the horizon, where laughter grows,
Every flower, a friend that knows.
In this humorous world, we all find our roles,
Where pollen is gold and laughter consoles.

The Connection of Colors

In a world of hues, they take their stand,
Bees and blooms, a whimsical band.
A daffodil twirls, all dressed in gold,
While a dandelion giggles, "You won't catch cold!"

A buzzing bumblebee tells a silly joke,
"Why do flowers always stay so bespoke?"
The petals laugh loud, "Because they adore,
When the sun comes out, they always want more!"

Butterflies flit with their painted wings,
Joining the chorus, oh, how joy sings!
Every bloom dances, some wiggly and proud,
Creating a canvas, where colors are loud.

From lavender trails to roses so bold,
The connection we share, a story retold.
In the garden of giggles, we weave and we play,
Funny, vibrant friendships bloom every day!

Flourishing Friendships

In a sunny patch, the daisies scheme,
Planning a party, oh what a dream!
Captain Bumblebee, with his wings all aglow,
Leads the parade in a fluffy sombrero!

The petunias giggle, they've dressed up so fine,
While the violet twins do a wiggly line.
"Join us!" they shout, "In our floral delight,
With nectar galore, we party all night!"

A grasshopper strummed on a leaf made of green,
While ladybugs danced in a radiant sheen.
With jubilant laughter, the garden does sway,
In hilarious chaos, they brighten the day.

As blossoms and buddies unite hand in hand,
Creating a fellowship, so wonderfully grand.
In this vibrant fiesta, each soul needs a friend,
In the whole world of flowers, the fun never ends!

The Language of Petals

In a garden, blooms have chatter,
Each whisper says, "Hey, you're the matter!"
With colors bold, they strut and sway,
While bees keep buzzing, "What's for play?"

Daisies giggle, while roses blush,
They compete in style, but never rush.
"Check my fragrance!" shouts a bright tulip,
The violets reply, "You need a cool trip!"

Sunflowers lean to catch a glimpse,
Of busy bees doing their frumpy flips.
"Look at me!" They buzz with glee,
But trip on petals, oh, what a spree!

At dusk, the blooms share silly tales,
Of daring winds and tiny fails.
The garden laughs in honest delight,
As the stars wink down on this floral night.

A Symphony of Bees

Bees in tuxedos, a formal parade,
Dancing and swirling, in sunlight they wade.
"Buzz, buzz, boogie!" they all sing loud,
While flowers clap, all gleeful and proud.

With nectar cups, they toast to the sun,
Each little sip, oh, what fun they have run!
"Have you tried this one?" says Shelton the bee,
"It's sweeter than candy, come have a spree!"

Swirling through petals, it's quite the scene,
They twirl in a ballet, oh so serene.
But whoops, there's a bump! A bee down he goes,
He shakes it off, grinning, "Just striking a pose!"

A symphony buzz ends with laughter and glee,
As flowers exhale, 'What funny decree!"
With a ballet of petals and a sweet honey sun,
These buzzing entertainers are always such fun!

Between Pollen and Petal

In a bustling garden, a party starts,
With petals on a dress, and bees with sweet hearts.
"Don't you dare touch my pollen!" a flower exclaims,
While bees give each other the silliest names.

"Pollen Popper!" buzzes a bee on the go,
While petals just giggle at this pollen show.
They dance in the sun, a colorful plight,
Tickling the wind with sheer delight.

With each tiny drop, a joke shared in flight,
Bees play hopscotch in the warm sunlight.
But a breeze takes a flower, uprooting the fun,
And petals start rolling—oh what a run!

"Get back here, petals!" the bees shout with glee,
In a whirlwind of colors, they chase with esprit.
Together they chuckle, a merry parade,
Between each pollen grain, this joy never fades!

Journeys of the Winged

Tiny aviators in quest for a taste,
Zipping through gardens, no moment to waste.
"Where's the party?" they buzz on a quest,
With wings all a-flutter, they're surely the best!

A butterfly flutters, showing off flair,
While bees zip past with a "Hey, unaware!"
"Look at me dance!" shouts a zippy little sprite,
But collides with a daisy, oh what a sight!

The flowers all cheer, their petals at play,
As winged jesters frolic throughout the day.
With laughter and pollen, they make a great team,
In this whimsical world, the flowers all beam.

As daylight wanes, they giggle for fun,
To the beat of the breezes, the races they run.
In the garden's embrace, they dream with delight,
These journeys of winged friends end with night.

The Golden Thread

In a garden where bees zany dance,
They tickle the flowers, give them a chance.
Pollen on their legs like confetti,
Making all blooms feel quite ready.

The butterflies gossip, wearing bright styles,
They glide and they flutter with cheeky smiles.
Each petal a canvas, each sip a delight,
Creating a ruckus from morning till night.

Ants march like soldiers, all orderly ranks,
Pointing out blooms like they're giving thanks.
But if you ask them, they just shrug it off,
Wiggling their butts, pretending to scoff.

And as they all dance to this zany tune,
The sun begins to hum a happy old tune.
With laughter and chaos, they paint the scene,
Nature's parade—oh, what a routine!

Nature's Love Letters

Dear Honey, a note from the sweet bumblebee,
Your nectar is the best, can't you see?
With every little kiss, I feel like a king,
Together we sway—let's dance and sing!

Dandelions blush, it's pure romance,
With each tiny gust, they spin and prance.
I'll sprinkle my wishes, you make them take flight,
Poof! Off they go in the soft evening light.

Oh, daffodils rise, wearing yellow so bright,
They wave to the sky, so eager for light.
With a wink and a nudge, they giggle a tune,
Whispering secrets beneath the ball moon.

And in this love fest, under stars so wide,
Nature's confessions cannot abide.
So here's to the blooms and all who adore,
Love letters in petals—who could ask for more?

Chronicles of the Bloom

Once upon a time, in a garden so grand,
A sprout had a dream, with its leaf-laden hand.
It yearned for the sun, it craved a sweet breeze,
And vowed to be more than just a few leaves.

The daisies debated, "Who's prettiest here?"
While the roses chimed in, "Don't shed a tear!"
It's all just a jest in this petally space,
They fight for the sun, with flowery grace.

Then came a storm, oh, what a wild scene,
With raindrops like marbles—so wet and obscene!
The tulips all wobbled, but laughed as they swayed,
In the chaos of nature, their fears allayed.

So here's to the blooms, with their funny little plots,
Turning the garden into giggle spots.
In the chronicles of life, let's not be too glum,
For laughter's the nectar from which we all come!

From Bud to Blossom

A bud on the vine had a plan so neat,
"To blossom today, oh, that'll be sweet!"
But the breeze played a prank, it gave it a shove,
And the bud tumbled out, like a free-flying dove.

"Oh no!" cried the bud, in a twisty retreat,
"You can't rush my growth, it's not quite complete!"
The sun just chuckled, "Let's see where you go,
Adventure awaits, come on, steal the show!"

With a flip and a flop, it landed all wrong,
Right next to a flower, with petals so strong.
"Hey bud, join the party, the fun's just begun!
Let's bloom and get wild, oh this'll be fun!"

And so they danced, till the stars waved goodnight,
With petals all tangled, in pure flower delight.
From bud to full bloom, life's just a big joke,
In the garden of laughter, where no one stays broke!

Melodies Beneath the Sun

Buzzy bees dance in midair,
With tiny hats and quite a flair.
They twirl around like they own the scene,
Singing songs in a sunny sheen.

Fluttering wings in a merry chase,
Chasing flowers at a lively pace.
Oh what fun, they're on a spree,
Making honey like it's free!

Gathering nectar, they form a line,
All for the sake of a sweet design.
With pollen pockets filled to the brim,
They leave the world a little less dim.

Each flower dons a polka-dot dress,
In this game of floral finesse.
As petals giggle in the warm sun,
Buzzy adventures have just begun!

Stars of the Garden

In the garden, a party erupts,
Where pollen-shakers chaotically jumped.
Dancing daisies with bright yellow hats,
Wiggling around with some cheeky chats.

Chubby caterpillars take center stage,
Spinning tales of a leafy age.
Ladybugs laugh, they can't sit still,
Fluttering in for the fun-filled thrill.

The sunflowers twirl, heads spinning 'round,
While shy lilacs peek from the ground.
"Oh, what's that?" the marigolds say,
A butterfly bouncing, leading the play!

As night drapes softly with a sprinkle of stars,
The critters retreat, starting their cars.
With dreams of petals and stems in their heads,
Tomorrow awaits for more antics to spread!

Flight and Flourish

Buzzing along like a silly parade,
The insects boast of their sweet escapade.
With tiny helmets and goggles on tight,
They zip through the air, oh what a sight!

Butterflies giggle, a flurry of color,
While beetles compete like a little school brawler.
"Catch me if you can!" a firefly teased,
But they all stopped when the daisies sneezed!

Petals flutter like flags in the breeze,
As pollinators land with effortless ease.
Each tiny traveler, a hero in flight,
Spreading joy on a flower-filled night.

They muddle and jive, a wacky ensemble,
Turning blossoms into a whimsical gamble.
With giggles and grace, they flourish so bold,
In nature's grand plan, a sight to behold!

Curves of the Cosmos

In the garden's heart, where laughter prevails,
A parade of petals sways, telling tales.
The bees buzz around in elaborate loops,
Joining the flowers, a meeting of troops.

With plucky worms wearing shades in style,
They groove to the rhythm, swaying all the while.
"Oh look!" crickets chirp with delight,
A dandelion blowing wishes all night!

Twisting, turning, arachnids weave,
Spinning stories that none would believe.
Each bloom a canvas, each hue a cheer,
Life's funny dance is precious and dear.

As evening descends, the stars all align,
The garden breaks out its best dance line.
Under the moon, they whirl and they twirl,
In this cosmic ballet, magic unfurls!

The Sweet Odyssey

In fields of yellow, bugs take flight,
They sip on nectar, oh what a sight!
With pollen pants, they dance and sway,
Like tiny partygoers, on a sunny day.

One bee got lost, took a wrong turn,
He buzzed to a cactus, now that's a burn!
A butterfly huffed, 'This isn't my scene,'
As he flapped away from a barbecue bean.

A ladybug laughed at a bumblebee's glide,
'You've got the moves, but where's your pride?'
They twirled 'round flowers, a colorful spree,
In this garden party, oh what glee!

With each little visit, they spread the cheer,
Turning boring blooms into laughter and beer!
With pollen in pockets, they strut and play,
In this sweet adventure, come join the fray!

Songs of the Sowers

High in the trees, the squirrels declare,
'We grow the best nuts, if you dare!'
They drop acorns everywhere,
Chasing butterflies, without a care.

The bees start buzzing their favorite tune,
While flowers sway to the rhythm of June.
With every flap and zing, they sing,
'Come join the fun that spring will bring!'

Grasshoppers hop, like they own the place,
Winking at blooms with a cheeky grace.
They're sowing seeds, and jokes, on the side,
As the dandelions giggle with pride.

Oh, what a symphony under the sun,
Where creatures gather, just having fun!
A party of nature, a wild, cheerful jam,
With all of us tuning in, oh ma'am!

Essence of the Arboreal

Under the branches, the whispers begin,
With whispers of critters, that tickle your chin.
The squirrels throw shade, while the raccoons laugh,
Trading tall tales, like it's a green craft.

A grasshopper croons about a lost sock,
Found in the bushes, just past the rock.
As ladybugs gossip, the ants roll their eyes,
Pointing at pigeons pretending to fly.

With every rustle and flutter in trees,
Branches embrace the whimsical breeze.
Nature keeps secrets that tickle the soul,
As sunlight spills laughter, making us whole.

Oh how we cherish these tales and more,
In this leafy land, we all want to explore!
Each critter a jester, oh what a sight,
In the essence of green, everything feels right!

The Dance of Delight

They gather at dusk, in a whirl of fun,
With fireflies twinkling, it's a nature run.
Crickets play tunes on their leafy stage,
As butterflies join in, full of courage and rage.

One ant wore a hat that was far too large,
He strutted about, leading the charge.
The lady beetles twirled in delight,
While beetles paired off, under the moonlight.

'Let's dance till dawn!' the chorus cried,
As blossoms swayed, they took it in stride.
The flowers shook petals, like glitter on skin,
In this raucous jamboree, let the show begin!

A frog played a fiddle, with style and flair,
His tune brought out laughter, floating in the air.
With every leap and buzzing sound,
The dance of delight spun round and round!

Nectarous News

Buzzing bees on morning news,
Sipping sweet, they skip their snooze.
Planting gossip, pollen's spread,
Garden chat in colors red.

Flower friends all laugh and sway,
With buzzing jokes that make their day.
"Did you hear what Gardener blurted?"
"Petals fluffed, but never curt-ed!"

Insects joining all the fun,
Swapping tales under the sun.
"Who's the prettiest on the block?"
"A daisy, but that's just talk!"

So when you see a busy bee,
Just know it's gossiping with glee.
Nature's news is never bland,
Sticky notes in flowerland.

Ballet of the Winged

With tippy toes, they take their flight,
Tiny dancers in the light.
Fluttering grace on petals bright,
A twirl here, a dip just right.

Robins chuckle at their show,
Pollen partners steal the glow.
The grass hums a wiggly tune,
As flowers nod while swaying soon.

Spinning circles, zigzag paths,
Bouncing off while nature laughs.
"Encore!" calls a dandelion,
With every spin, they keep on tryin'.

The curtain falls with buzzing cheer,
A standing swarm to end the year.
With wings all tired, but hearts so wide,
The daytime ballet, they're the pride.

The Blooming Passport

Stamped in colors all around,
Every flower is a traveling ground.
Petals sharing tales from afar,
"I once danced with a shooting star!"

A ladybug checks her list,
Counting blooms that she has kissed.
"Off to orchids, here I go,
Exploring places we all know!"

With each pollen grain packed tight,
They set off with delight in flight.
"Next stop's the tulip's sunny land,
You bring nectar, I bring sand!"

So gather 'round, each bee and bug,
With passports full, they love to hug.
Adventure waits in every breeze,
In the world of blooms, they're never freeze!

Wandering Whispers

In the garden, whispers roam,
Little secrets, not far from home.
"Did you see the bees' new dance?
They've gone wild in a pollen trance!"

Flowers giggle, sharing news,
"I heard they wear the latest shoes!"
A tulip twirls with glee and sass,
"Let's show them our lawn-mower class!"

Winds carry tales from spring to fall,
Where butterflies have lunch with all.
"Bring your nectar, it's a feast,
Our buzzing pals, they like it least!"

With every gust, joy never halts,
Nature's whispers, filled with faults.
So join the laughter, take your cue,
In the garden, there's fun for you!

Secrets of Succulence

In gardens where the bees do frolic,
A flower whispers, "How quite symbolic!"
With sugary nectar, a secret delight,
Bees buzz in a dance, oh what a sight!

The petals unfolding, in colors so bright,
They giggle and wink in the warm sunlight.
"I'm more delicious!" the daisies contest,
As the buzzing brigade puts their taste buds to test.

Through fragrant confusion, they zip and they zoom,
Pollinating gossip, creating a bloom.
"Whose pollen is better?" they natter and tease,
As laughter escapes through the rustling leaves.

So here's to the flowers, both silly and sweet,
With nectar so rich, just a little you'll eat.
In fields of delight, their secrets unfold,
In the buzz of the honey, the stories are told!

Connection through the Cosmos

In the realm of the flowers, where stardust does play,
Bees zoom like rockets, in a cosmic ballet.
"Hey flower!" they shout, "You shine like a star!"
"Buzz on, dear friend, you're my favorite by far!"

With pollen as currency, they barter and trade,
As colors collide in a glittery parade.
The daisies laugh hard, as the cosmos conspire,
"To be picked by a bee is a true badge of fire!"

Galactic connections in scent and in hue,
Pollinators chuckle, "We're a bright crew!"
With each tiny drop, they spread laughter and cheer,
As flowers bloom boldly, "Oh look, we're all here!"

From purple to gold, in a dizzying swirl,
They twirl and they whirl, in a pollen-filled whirl.
So tip your nectar glass, and toast to the skies,
For in this wild game, everyone flies!

The Call of the Wildflower

Oh wildflower, dancing in the breeze,
With petals like laughter, you bring delight with ease.
You beckon the bumble with a jovial jig,
As he does a cha-cha, oh what a gig!

"Come close, little keeper of cosmic delight!"
"I have nectar so sweet, it'll make you take flight!"
The bumblebee chuckles, "I love this sweet deal,
Let's mingle and wiggle, oh what a thrill!"

In a twist of their hearts, they share silly tales,
Of gardens and forests, and flower-filled trails.
With giggles and grins, they pollinate souls,
Creating a symphony of funny flower roles.

The wildflower's laughter is heard all around,
"Buzz along, little one, let your joy abound!"
In a chorus of colors, they join in a cheer,
For with every new visit, the fun reappears!

A Journey Written in Wings

The butterflies flaunt in the soft summer sun,
While bees swarm around, and the fun's just begun.
"Oh, look at you, fashionista!" they tease,
"Your wings are like art; you do as you please!"

In gardens they gather, a colorful mess,
With giggles and wiggles, they relish the dress.
"Let's make this a picnic!" the pink blooms declare,
As wildflowers hum, "We'll dance without a care!"

Each flower rejoices with petals held high,
As they serve up the nectar, under bright azure sky.
The bees bring the music, while butterflies sway,
Creating a ruckus, all night, all day!

So here's to the travelers with wings so free,
Spreading joy and laughter, as sweet as can be!
In gardens of whimsy, they take to the air,
Writing delightful stories, all beyond compare!

Mosaic of Life

A busy bee with a tiny hat,
Wears a tie made of soft, fuzzy chat.
He dances a jig on a daisy's face,
Spreading cheer in a floral race.

Butterflies flutter in a grand parade,
With wings of glitter, their colors displayed.
They gossip of nectar and sugary treats,
Sipping with laughter on sweet, sticky feats.

Grasshoppers jump with a humorous flair,
Cracking jokes that hang in the air.
A ladybug chuckles, her spots all aglow,
While ants march in step, stealing the show.

In this garden where giggles abound,
Life weaves a tapestry vibrant and sound.
Each buzz and flap tells a tale with glee,
In the mosaic of life, come laugh with me!

The Silent Communion

In the hush of morn, bees hold a chat,
Exchanging sweet secrets where blossoms sat.
With tiny blabber, they sip and they spy,
While ants in a line just roll on by.

The tulips giggle, their petals all bright,
Sharing gossip of bugs through the night.
"Why do we bloom?" asks a shy little sprout,
"To catch all the buzz, of course!" they shout.

Bees wear their shades in the golden sun's glow,
While snails take a sip at a slow-paced show.
A butterfly swoops, thinking it's a race,
But trips on a petal, what a silly face!

With each quiet hum, they share and they grin,
Finding humor in every little win.
In this silent symphony, laughter is bliss,
A ballet of buds, wouldn't want to miss!

Petals in Flight

Dandelion fluff takes off in the breeze,
Scattering laughter as light as can be.
"Catch me if you can!" it cheekily yells,
While clover folks giggle, casting their spells.

Bees on a mission in tuxedos so neat,
Dance like they're grooving to a funky beat.
With pollen as bling, they twirl and they spin,
"Have you seen my dance moves?" they boast with a grin.

The flowers lean in, whispering jokes,
About buzzing and blooming, and silly hopes.
A daisy declares, "I'm the queen of this hive!"
With petals outstretched, oh, how she'll thrive!

In this garden of whimsy, where laughter takes flight,
Each moment is golden, a pure delight.
Petals in the wind serve giggles anew,
In a joyful ballet, just me and you!

Radiance of the Realm

Sunshine beams down, a playful hello,
As flowers act silly, putting on a show.
The tulips wear glasses to block out the light,
While daisies discuss who's the star of the night.

Buzzy brigade in a whirlwind of fun,
Doing the tango, they're second to none.
A butterfly flutters, brandishing flair,
While blooms stand in awe of its colorful air.

The lavender laughs, with a voice sweet and clear,
"Join my dance party, just don't spill your beer!"
While sunflowers nod, fresh jokes to they spread,
As giggles abound amidst petals all red.

In the realm of the joyous where laughter prevails,
Each critter and flower tells funny tales.
Radiance glimmers, in colors so bold,
In this garden of smiles, come laugh, be gold!

A Caravan of Colors

In the garden, blooms a show,
Bees in shades that steal the glow.
Pollen suits and tiny hats,
Buzzing laughter, clumsy bats!

Butterflies in disco moves,
Chasing scents, they find their grooves.
With every flap, they shake and sway,
Making flowers shout hooray!

Ladybugs join in the fun,
Rolling 'round just like the sun.
Spreading joy with polka dots,
Who knew plants had such cool spots?

Nature's jesters, here they come,
Pollination: the garden's drum.
So grab a drink and take a seat,
This vibrant show can't be beat!

The Artistry of Sweet Interludes

Amidst the petals, sweet delight,
A wiggly worm takes off in flight.
Dancing nectar drips with charm,
Sipping pollen, it's quite the balm!

Each bee a dancer, fancy spins,
Noticing the fun never ends.
With pollen smeared on every wing,
Who knew flowers could make you sing?

Hummingbirds with flashy flair,
Zipping past without a care.
Sipping sweets and buzzing loud,
Perfecting moves to draw a crowd!

Nature's theater, what a show,
With every taste, the colors glow.
So raise a glass to those who roam,
In this garden, they call home!

Whispers of the Wild

In fields where critters roam about,
A rabbit sneezes, there's no doubt!
With every hop, it scents the air,
Flowers giggle without a care.

Buzzy friends in frantic chase,
Chasing shadows, keeping pace.
With sticky feet, they land in style,
Pollen on their noses, such a smile!

Grasshoppers join the silly spree,
Riding breezes, wild and free.
Jokers of the summer sun,
Painting colors, having fun!

Each pollinator knows the game,
In this wild, there's no shame.
So here's a cheer for all involved,
In nature's mess, the problems solved!

Nectar's Dance

Amidst the blooms, a party swells,
Where insects gossip, share their tales.
Nectar drips like honeyed rain,
And butterflies join in the refrain!

With clumsy feet and dreams of gold,
The little guests seem brave and bold.
Each little sip, a taste of fun,
As petals spin beneath the sun!

Dragonflies buzz like tiny planes,
Zooming around in playful gains.
Who knew such joy could bring a sting,
In the garden where they sing?

So let us raise a toast today,
To all the colorful ballet!
For in this dance of sweet delight,
Every heart can take to flight!

Notes from Nature's Palette

In fields of green, they hum and buzz,
A dance of legs with little fuzz.
With nectar sweet as candy treats,
They swarm round flowers, moving their beats.

Each bloom's a stage, a floral jest,
The bumblebee thinks it's a guest.
It sips and spins, then off it flies,
While petals giggle in bright disguise.

But beware the thorns that sometimes bite,
A prickly joke in morning light.
The daisies laugh, low to the ground,
While pollen chuckles, all around.

In this wild show, no need for grace,
Just frolic free in nature's space.
Each color swirls, a playful sight,
As pollen parties carry on all night.

Journey of the Fragrant

It starts at dawn with scents galore,
A fragrant trail, we can't ignore.
The bees, they buzz, like tiny cars,
They're off to find the loveliest jars.

With wings that flap like crazy fans,
They sip from blooms, ignoring plans.
Each petal's wink is all it takes,
To lure them in with sweet mistakes.

They fumble often, spill the drink,
These little chaps just seem to think,
That every flower's a buffet grand,
With pollen pies, all unplanned.

So on they zoom, with laughs and spins,
A circus show where everyone wins.
In nature's dance, they make their mark,
As flowers cheer in the sunlight's spark.

In the Arms of Flora

In gentle arms, the blossoms sway,
Their petals shout, 'Come out to play!'
The bugs parade, a costume show,
In vibrant hues, they steal the glow.

The ladybugs in polka dots,
Are strutting proud, connecting spots.
While ants march by, on little quests,
In search of treats, they're such good pests.

One big bee tripped over a rose,
He laughed it off, 'Who needs more woes?'
With wobbly hops, he claims his throne,
In nature's court, he's never alone.

In joyful chaos, the garden hums,
As blooms burst forth with silly drums.
They share a laugh, a fragrant tease,
In flora's arms, life's sweetest breeze.

Fading Footprints of the Winged

With tiny feet, they leave their marks,
On petals bright, their little sparks.
They flit and flutter, a silly game,
While sunshine laughs and calls their name.

The wind plays tricks, a cheeky spree,
As butterflies dance with glee.
They sip from blooms, then laugh aloud,
While flowers blush, all bright and proud.

But oops! One bee forgot his way,
He ended up in potpourri's bay.
With scents so strong, he starts to spin,
'This isn't nectar,' he says with a grin.

As colors fade in dusk's embrace,
The winged ones frolic in their space.
With happy chirps and sleepy sighs,
They dream of blooms 'neath twilight skies.

www.ingramcontent.com/pod-product-compliance
Lightning Source LLC
Chambersburg PA
CBHW051659160426
43209CB00004B/963